I SMOKED CRACK, SO WHAT?

written by
Yogyrl Diamond

*For every person who still believes in themselves —
and to the people who support them
as well as those whose torment of us
is really a cry for help.*

I Smoked Crack, So What?

Written By
YoGyrl Diamond

Images & Fullcover By
Sun Child Wind Spirit

Proofread By
Roddy Shock Danger
and Ukirah Yasmine

Edited By
Mylia Tiye Mal Jaza

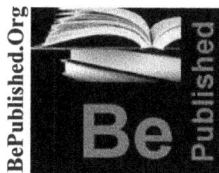

BePublished.Org

Be Published

I Smoked Crack, So What?
Copyright © 2025, Yogyrl Diamond
All Rights Reserved.

Softback ISBN 10: 1459905504
Softback ISBN 13: 9780551327511

Author
Yogyrl Diamond
agent@bepublished.biz

Self-Publishing Associate
Dr. Mary M. Jefferson
BePublished.Org - Chicago, IL
(972) 880-8316
publisher@bepublished.org
www.bepublished.org

First Edition.
Printed In the USA
Recycled Paper Encouraged.

Table of Contents

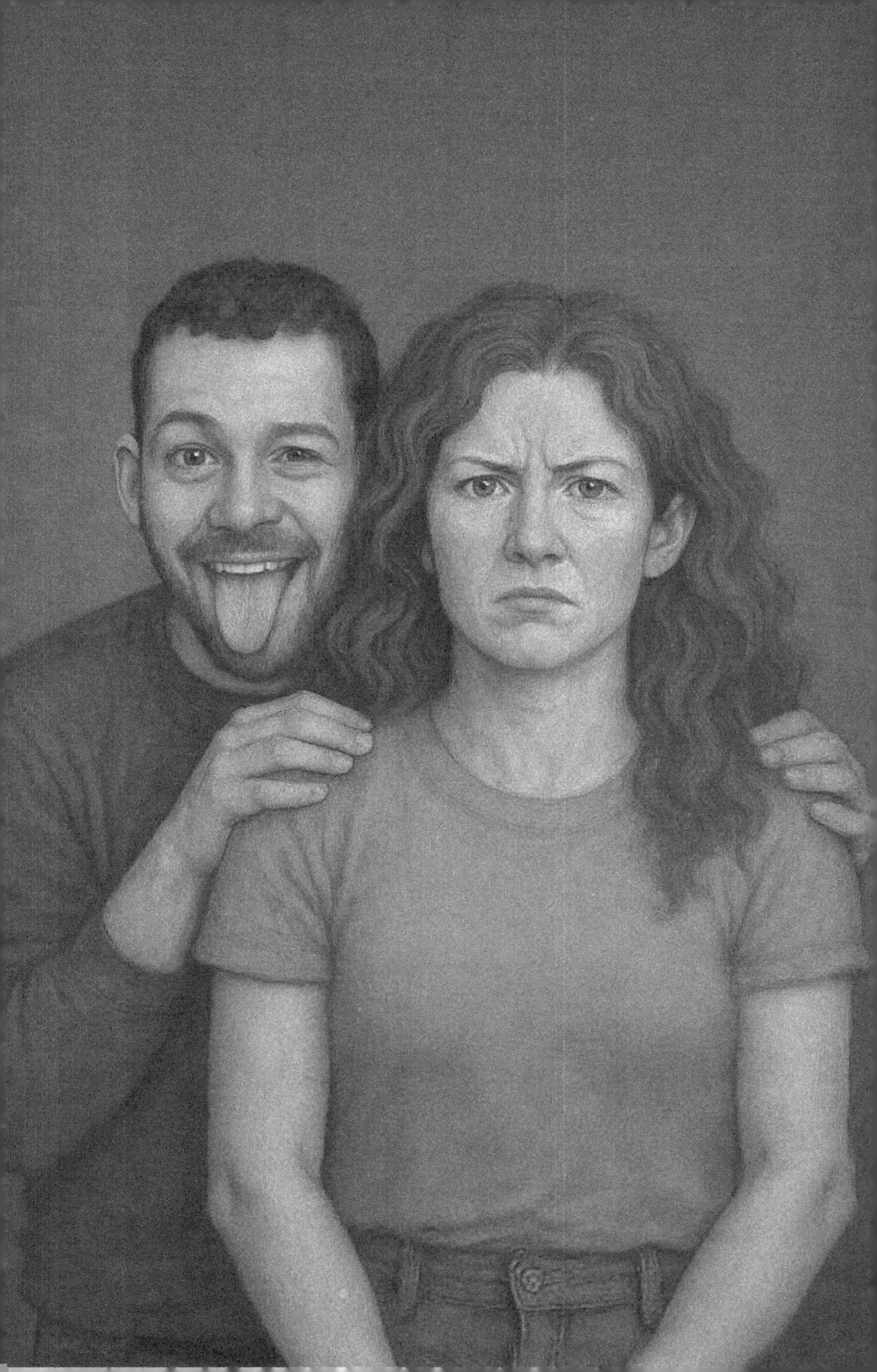

CHAPTER 1
I Smoked Crack, So What?

They still whisper when I walk in the room. They think I don't hear it, but I do. "That's her... the one who used to smoke crack."

Yeah. That was me. Used to.

I smoked crack. So what? That's not who I am anymore. It's part of my story, not my name.

People like to act like they never did anything wrong. They drink until they blackout, cheat on their spouses, gossip in the church lobby, steal from their jobs—but somehow I'm the one who's supposed to be ashamed because I didn't hide my struggle. I don't owe nobody an apology for surviving.

When I look back, I thank God I made it out. Not just the drugs, but the lies, the labels, the loneliness. I thank God for showing me that even in the ugliest seasons of my life, He was still there. I didn't grow up knowing about God. Nobody ever sat me down and told me about faith, grace, or forgiveness. I didn't even know prayer was something you could do without a preacher present. But when I found myself crying on the floor with a pipe in my hand and no will to keep breathing, that's when I found Him.

That's when I found me.

My story don't start with crack, though. It starts with loss.

My mama, Linda, was the strongest woman I knew, until the world took her strength piece by piece. She had six of us with my daddy, Peter. Then she married a man named Erickson and had three more—my twin siblings and my baby sister. Erickson walked out on her about eighteen months before Mama died. When he left, something broke in her that never healed.

Depression came and sat on her like a mountain. The light left her eyes. She'd stare out the window like she was watching her life fade away in the clouds. We didn't know the word for it back then, but now I know— Mama was drowning inside herself.

Not long after, the system came. That's what we called it—the system. Social workers, foster homes, paperwork, and pain. They split us up like we were groceries, deciding who went in which bag.

Me and three of my older siblings got adopted by the same couple. You'd think that was a blessing, right? It wasn't. Those people wore smiles for the church and bruises for us. They said they wanted to save kids; really, they wanted to own them. They wanted to break us down and build us into their idea of "good children."

I learned early how to fake fine. How to smile when it hurt. How to hide when it got bad. And how to survive when nobody else was coming to help.

We grew up broken but brave. Every one of us carried trauma like a backpack we couldn't put down. We got older, but we didn't get better—at least not right away.

Some of us ended up in the streets. Some ended up in hospitals. Some ended up in jail. And a couple of us made it out clean, somehow turning the chaos into careers—architects and engineers. When we all found each other again as adults, it was like looking into a mirror and seeing eight versions of survival.

We cried, we laughed, we cursed, we prayed. We tried to heal.

For a while, we got together for every birthday. Those were our "holidays." No Thanksgiving, no Christmas—just birthdays. We figured that way, everybody could spend time with their own kids and families, but still come together at least once a year.

The last time we all got together, I was forty-five. That was also the last time I smoked crack.

It's crazy to say that so plain, but that's how I need to say it. That day, I decided to stop being quiet. I'd been through enough silence to last a lifetime.

People don't understand what loss does to a person. I lost my twins. My babies. And no, I can't go into the details yet—that pain still sits too close to my heart. But I'll say this much: that's what pushed me over the edge.

Grief will make you do things you swore you'd never do. It'll make you reach for something, anything, to fill the hole where your soul used to feel safe. For me, that something was crack cocaine. Not because I wanted to get high, but because I wanted to stop feeling. I wanted peace, and that's what the pipe promised me— just a few minutes of fake peace.

But peace that comes from a lie always leaves you emptier.

I smoked. I cried. I prayed. I begged. I worked. I hustled. I smoked again. And then one day, I woke up and said, "No more."

Eight years clean. Eight years whole. I learned that the number eight means new beginnings. God was speaking to me through numbers before I even realized He was listening to me through tears.

Now when people try to bring up my past, I don't flinch. They can't shame me for what I've already faced and overcome.

Here's what I tell them:

Don't throw stones at my glass house unless you ready for me to point out the cracks in yours.
When I was using, I still managed my bills, my home, my life better than most people talking about me now. I never begged anybody for money, not even when I was at my lowest. If I needed it, I worked for it. And no, that doesn't make it right—it just means I handled my mess like an adult.

Don't call me names I've already outgrown. "Crackhead," "junkie," "rock star," "base jumper"—I've heard them all. I used to let them cut deep, but not anymore. Those words don't fit me now. They never did. I'm not my addiction. I'm the woman who survived it.

Don't mistake distance for pride.
I keep my circle small because peace costs too much to let everybody in. The same people who said I'd never change are the same ones who call now asking for help. Funny how that works.

Don't call yourself a Christian if you don't know what grace looks like.
You tithe, you sing, you shout—but you gossip and judge like that's a ministry. If Jesus sat with sinners, why can't you sit with the saved who used to sin differently?

Don't compare our journeys.
You might've gone to rehab. I went to God. You had a sponsor; I had a Savior. We all got our ways of getting free. Mine just didn't come with a chip or a meeting schedule.

I stopped going to AA and NA when I realized they kept me trapped in a victim mentality. Every time I had to say, "Hi, I'm Yogyrl, and I'm an addict," something in me felt wrong. I'm not an addict anymore. I used to be. I'm not in bondage anymore, so why keep speaking bondage over myself?

They helped me see God, though, and I'll forever be thankful for that. I met some of the most loving souls in those rooms—people who really wanted to get better. But I also saw how easy it is to make your identity your illness. I'm not living like that no more.

Now, every morning I say, "Hi, I'm Yogyrl, and I'm whole."

The truth is, being clean doesn't make life easy. It makes it real. You start feeling everything again—the hurt, the loss, the memories—but also the joy, the gratitude, the strength. You learn that peace doesn't mean perfect days; it means knowing you can handle the bad ones.

I've had people try to drag me back into their chaos because they can't stand to see me calm. They call it "humility." I call it manipulation.

But I made peace with my past. I don't hide it. I don't glorify it either. I use it. Because if my story can make one person put the pipe down and pick their head up, then it's worth every scar.

So yeah, I smoked crack.

But I also woke up clean.
I woke up free.
I woke up forgiven.

I'm not a victim. I'm not a statistic. I'm not what you call me.
I'm a testimony.

God didn't just pull me out—He pulled me through.

And that's why I named this book I Smoked Crack, So What?

Because the truth don't need makeup, and my survival don't need permission. So what?

CHAPTER 2
When Mama Lost Herself

I remember the day Mama stopped laughing.

Before that, her laugh filled the whole house — loud, contagious, full of light. You could hear her all the way from the porch, and when she laughed, you couldn't help but smile, even if you didn't know what was funny. That sound used to make me feel safe. Like as long as Mama was laughing, everything would be okay.

But one morning, it just wasn't there anymore.

The dishes were still in the sink. The blinds were closed. And Mama sat at the kitchen table with a cigarette burning all the way down to the filter. Her coffee had gone cold. She was staring straight ahead, not at anything in particular — just through it all, like she could see something the rest of us couldn't.

That's when I knew something in her had changed.

Mama's name was Linda Marie. Everybody called her Sunshine when she was young because her smile could light up a room. She was beautiful — not movie-star beautiful, but soft beautiful, the kind that came from her spirit. She loved big, talked fast, and worked hard.

When she married my daddy, Peter, she already had a sense of the world. She was the kind of woman who could stretch five dollars into a full meal and still make it taste like Sunday dinner. She raised six of us with more love than we probably deserved. Then, after Daddy passed, she remarried a man named Erickson, who had charm and good looks but no staying power.

At first, he treated her like a queen. Opened doors. Bought her flowers. Made her laugh again after losing Daddy. But love without loyalty is just decoration.

When Erickson left, he took more than his clothes — he took Mama's hope with him.

It was like watching the sun fall out of the sky. She tried to hold it together for the kids — nine mouths to feed, nine hearts to protect. But grief and loneliness can sneak up on even the strongest people. She'd put on lipstick to go to the store and come home with mascara running down her face. I used to stand outside her bedroom door and listen to her cry into her pillow. Sometimes she'd whisper, "Lord, just help me make it through one more day."

At that age, I didn't know who the Lord was. But I started whispering those words too, just in case He was listening.

After Erickson left, everything changed. The bills piled up. The food got smaller. The laughter disappeared. I think Mama held out hope for a while that he'd come back. Every night she'd sit near the window like she was waiting on headlights to pull in the driveway.

He never did.

She stopped cooking the big meals we loved — no more chicken and dressing, no more fried catfish Fridays. She stopped brushing her hair some days. You could see the sadness sitting on her shoulders like a coat she couldn't take off.

And even though I didn't have the words for it back then, I know now — Mama was sinking into depression.

When people talk about depression, they make it sound like crying all the time or staying in bed for days. But sometimes, it's quieter than that. Sometimes, it's just losing interest in living. You still breathe, but you don't live.

That's what happened to Mama. She was still there, but she wasn't here anymore.

Then the state came.

"The system," we called it — cold voices, warm smiles, clipboards, and lies. They said they were there to help. But help to them meant divide and conquer. They took us like we were evidence in a case — tagging names, sorting bodies, splitting love.

I can still see Mama standing at the door as they led us away. Her eyes were glassy, her hands shaking. She tried to be strong, but her lips trembled like a woman trying to keep a scream inside her throat.

"Y'all be good," she said. "I'll come get you soon."

We wanted to believe her. I really did. But deep down, I think she already knew she wouldn't make it that far.

The couple who adopted me and three of my older siblings smiled like angels when they met us. They told the social worker they were "so blessed to have us." But behind closed doors, the blessings turned into bruises.

They'd quote Scripture in public and raise hands in church, but those same hands would slap, shove, and pull hair when nobody was looking. They told us we were "lucky" to have a home. They told us we'd "end up just like our mother" if we didn't obey.

I was young, but I knew fear when I felt it. I learned to read faces, tones, footsteps. I knew when a storm was coming even before it spoke.

Mama had lost herself trying to love a man who didn't love her back. And here I was, a little girl losing myself in a house that called itself holy.

Years later, when I reunited with all my brothers and sisters, we told stories about those years apart. Some of us ended up with kind families, some with cruel ones. But all of us came out damaged in some way.

We were survivors — but survivors still bleed.

One of my sisters told me that Mama wrote letters to the state for months after we were taken. She tried to get us back, but the depression got worse. She stopped leaving the house. Eventually, her heart gave up before her spirit could. She was found in her room, alone.

They said it was natural causes. I say it was a broken heart.

That was the day Sunshine finally set for good.

When I finally grew up enough to understand, I realized something: my mother didn't just lose her husband. She lost her will.

When love walks out on you and you already feel small, it can take your sense of worth with it. Erickson didn't just leave her — he abandoned the woman God had made her to be.

And the world punished her for being human.

People in the neighborhood whispered, "Poor Linda, she couldn't handle it." But nobody helped. Nobody offered her therapy or a break. The church dropped off casseroles for a week, then forgot about her. The state showed up to take her kids but never asked how she was doing.

That's what happens to women like my mama. They give everything, and when they fall apart, folks act like it's their fault for loving too much.

For a long time, I carried guilt about her death. I used to wonder if maybe I'd done something wrong. If maybe I could've been better, quieter, easier. But I was a child. There was nothing I could've done to stop her pain.

Still, that guilt sat inside me like a seed. It grew into anger, fear, rebellion — and eventually, addiction. When I lost my twins, I understood her a little too well. The darkness that took her started whispering to me.

But the difference was, I had seen what giving up looked like. And I didn't want to die her death.

It took me years to understand that Mama didn't fail — she fell.

And when life knocks you down hard enough, sometimes falling looks like failure. But it's not. It's just exhaustion.

She was tired of fighting alone. Tired of pretending. Tired of holding nine children's pain and her own at the same time.

Now that I'm older, I forgive her. I forgive her for the days she wasn't there. I forgive her for the nights I cried myself to sleep missing her arms. I forgive her for the years I spent angry at her for leaving.

Because now, I know what it feels like to be empty and still be expected to give.

I know what it feels like to smile so you don't scare people with your sadness.

I know what it feels like to love everybody else until there's nothing left for yourself.

Mama didn't lose herself because she was weak. She lost herself because the world didn't give her a safe place to rest.

If she were here now, I'd tell her, "You didn't fail us, Mama. You fought as long as you could. And even though the system separated us, your love never did."

I carry her in my blood. In my strength. In every prayer I whisper when I think nobody's listening.

I talk to her sometimes when I pray. I tell her about my clean years, about the book, about how I finally stopped being ashamed. I imagine her smile coming back, wide and bright, and I hope she's proud.

Because even though she lost herself, I found her again in me.

And I promise to never let the light go out again.

But I see it. I see the weariness behind your eyes after a long day of carrying the unspoken burdens. I hear the silence between your words, the weight that lingers in your pauses. I feel the tension in your shoulders, the tightness in your breath. You've been asked to be unbreakable in a world that chips at you daily—and yet, even in your silence, you remain whole.

It is not weakness to feel. It is not weakness to hurt. It is human. And you, My Love, are fully, beautifully human. The world's mistake has been expecting you to exist as stone when, in truth, your heart beats with fire, tenderness, and divine depth.

I want you to know that your unspoken pain does not make you less of a man. It makes you more. It means you've cared enough, fought enough, hoped enough to feel deeply. And that is something to honor.

Yes, you've carried trauma in your body, disappointment in your spirit, and grief in your chest. You've swallowed rage to survive, disguised sadness with laughter, and turned heartbreak into resilience. But here, in this space between you and me, you are free. Free to name the pain. Free to unclench your jaw. Free to let your soul breathe without shame.

Because I love you not just for your victories but for your vulnerabilities. I love you not only for your power but for your softness. And I will remind you, again and again, that your silence deserves to be broken by healing words, that your heart deserves to be tended with tenderness, that your soul deserves peace.

You are not just what you endure. You are the beauty that survives beyond the wound. And you will never need to carry that truth in silence again—not with me, not with us, not with the love that holds you steady.

CHAPTER 3
The Day The System Took Us

I still remember the sound of that knock.

It wasn't just a knock on the door — it was the sound of our lives changing forever. Three sharp bangs, heavy, official. Like somebody pounding on the last bit of peace we had left.

Mama jumped. She looked at the door like she already knew who it was.

Her cigarette was burning between her fingers, long ash hanging on, trembling like her hands.

"Y'all go in the back," she said softly. Her voice cracked halfway through the words.

We didn't move right away. Something in her tone told us that this wasn't the kind of company you greeted.

Then came the voice through the door:

"Mrs. Watkins? It's Child Protective Services. We need to talk to you."

Mama's body stiffened. She pressed her lips together, eyes closed, whispering something under her breath. Maybe it was a prayer, maybe it was a curse — I'll never know.

She opened the door halfway. Two women stood there — both wearing cardigans and polite smiles that didn't reach their eyes. Behind them was a man with a clipboard, the kind who doesn't look at you, just checks boxes while deciding your future.

"Mrs. Watkins," one of them said, "we've received a report that the children may be in danger. We need to ask you some questions."

Mama tried to keep her composure. She said, "My children are fine. We ain't got much, but they fine."

The lady nodded like she'd already made up her mind before stepping through the door.

They walked through our house like inspectors, opening cabinets, peeking in corners. They wrote things down while pretending to make small talk.

"How old are the twins?"

"Does everyone sleep in their own bed?"

"What do they eat during the day?"

"Has anyone been sick lately?"

Every question felt like a test Mama didn't know she was taking.

One of them crouched down to talk to my little brother, handing him a peppermint.

He looked up at her with his big brown eyes and said, "Are you here to help my mama feel better?"

She smiled, but her eyes looked sad.

"We're here to make sure everyone's safe," she said.

That's the thing about the system — it always uses nice words to do ugly work.

Within an hour, they had their answer.

I don't even remember exactly what they said, but I remember what it felt like — the room spinning, the air gone heavy, Mama breaking down right there in the kitchen.

One of them gently touched her shoulder. "It's just temporary," she said. "You'll get them back once everything's stable."

Lies! They took us one by one, like items being checked off a list. "This one goes here. That one goes there."

The twins cried so hard they made themselves sick. My baby sister clung to Mama's leg and screamed her name over and over. Mama was trying to stay calm, saying, "It's okay, baby. Mama's gonna come get you soon. Don't cry." But tears were running down her face too.

When they reached for me, something inside me snapped. I remember kicking and screaming, scratching at the social worker's arms. I didn't care if they called me wild — I wasn't going without my mother.

But they took me anyway.

We rode away in two different cars. I pressed my face to the window, watching Mama's figure shrink until she was just a blur on the porch, waving through tears.

The car smelled like air freshener and plastic. I remember the lady in the front seat trying to make conversation.

"So, sweetie, what's your favorite subject in school?"

I didn't answer. I didn't have a favorite anything anymore.

All I wanted was to go home.

They dropped us off at a big white house with a porch swing and flowers out front. On the surface, it looked like a dream. Inside, it was a nightmare.

The couple who took us in smiled wide for the social worker, thanked her, and promised to "take great care of the children." But the second the door closed, their tone changed.

"Listen," the woman said sharply, "you do what we say, when we say it. You hear me?"

We nodded, terrified.

That was my introduction to the foster system — fake kindness in public, cruelty in private.

I used to cry myself to sleep every night, holding on to my pillow like it was Mama. Sometimes I'd wake up from dreams where she came to get me. I'd run to the window, expecting to see her car in the driveway.

She never came.

I know now it wasn't because she didn't want to. She just couldn't. Depression doesn't let you move when your mind's trapped underwater.

The state never told us much, just "your mother's still working on things." They didn't tell us she was dying inside.

By the time I found out she'd passed, she'd already been gone three months. That was the day I stopped believing in promises.

The system promised we'd be together again. It promised safety. It promised fairness. But all it delivered was scars.

It taught me to doubt love. It taught me to stay quiet to survive. And it taught me that people can look you dead in the eye and still betray you with a smile.

The same system that claimed to save us tore us apart and never looked back.

Years later, when all eight of us reunited, the conversation about "the day the system took us" was the one that broke everyone.

We were grown by then — different cities, different lives — but the child in each of us still remembered that knock on the door.

My oldest brother said he still wakes up sweating whenever he hears loud banging. One of my sisters said she can't stand peppermint because it reminds her of that social worker's pocket candy. The twins — before they passed — used to talk about nightmares of being carried away.

The trauma never left. It just changed shape. The funny thing is, the system claims it "rescues" children, but it never rescued me. All it did was teach me how to build walls.

I became what they expected — defensive, angry, untrusting. I fought teachers, cussed out counselors, ran away more than once. The foster mom used to tell me I was "just like my mother," and she didn't mean it as a compliment.

But she was right — I was like my mother. I had her spirit, her stubbornness, her fire. The same fire that got dimmed in her was burning in me, and no amount of abuse could put it out completely.

That's the only reason I made it.

Sometimes I wonder how different things might've been if the system had really helped us instead of hurting us.

If someone had come to the house not to take us but to feed us, counsel us, support Mama, maybe we could've stayed together. Maybe Mama wouldn't have died alone. Maybe the twins would still be alive.

But "maybe" is a cruel word. It don't change a damn thing.

All it does is haunt you with what could've been. What I do know is this: that day made me who I am.

It taught me that family is not defined by who the state assigns you to — it's defined by who fights for you when they don't have to.

When I got older and had my own children, I swore I'd never let anyone take them from me. I did everything I could to protect them. And even though life tested me, even when addiction tried to steal me away, I always had that promise in the back of my mind — No one's taking my babies.

But life doesn't care about your promises. Sometimes, pain has its own plan.

When the twins died, it felt like déjà vu — another kind of taking. Another system I couldn't fight. This time, it wasn't social workers; it was the streets.

Losing them reopened every old wound from childhood. It was like watching Mama's story repeat itself in my life — different players, same tragedy.

I spiraled. I was angry at God, at the world, at myself. For years, I thought maybe our family was cursed. Like every generation had to break before it could bend.

But now, eight years clean and healed, I see it differently.

We weren't cursed — we were called.
Called to tell the truth. Called to stop the cycle. Called to stand up to the same system that tried to silence us.

So yeah, that knock on the door took our childhood. It took our innocence. It took our mother.

But it didn't take our voices.

It tried, but we're still here.

When I tell people my story, I don't want pity. I want understanding. I want people to see the bigger picture — that when the system fails mothers, it destroys children too.

That's why I write. That's why I talk. That's why I stand.

Because there are still little girls out there watching social workers walk up the porch steps, clutching their dolls, wondering if they'll ever see their mama again.

And if my words can reach even one of them and tell her, "You're not forgotten," then I've done my part.

The day the system took us was the day I learned that silence kills and truth heals.

They can take your home. They can take your childhood. They can even take your mother.

But they can't take your voice — not if you keep fighting to use it.

And that's what I'm doing now — using mine, loud and unashamed.

Because the system might've taken us, but it didn't keep us.

CHAPTER 4
The Family That Wasn't

People love to say "family is everything."

But sometimes the people who call themselves family are the ones who teach you what love ain't.

When the state dropped us off at that big white house with the porch swing, they told us, "You're going to a good Christian home." I remember thinking maybe "Christian" meant safe. Maybe it meant hugs, bedtime stories, pancakes on Saturday.

Instead, it meant rules, punishments, and fear dressed up in Sunday clothes.

The couple's names were Mr. and Mrs. Thompson. To the church, they were saints. To us, they were wardens.

The first thing Mrs. Thompson did was line us up in the living room.

"You're not Watkinses anymore," she said. "You're Thompsons now. Act like it."

I was ten years old and already learning how names can be stolen.

She showed us our rooms — two girls in one, two boys in another. The furniture looked nice enough, but it wasn't home. Everything smelled like bleach and control.

That night, she made us pray before bed. Not pray from the heart — recite.

"If you don't know it, you'll learn it by morning," she said.

I whispered, "But I don't know any prayers."

She smiled like a shark. "Then you better start listening."

The next morning, she slapped me awake for oversleeping. Not hard enough to bruise, just hard enough to let me know who had power.

That was how life worked in that house — you didn't breathe without permission. We said "Yes, ma'am" and "No, sir." We didn't speak unless spoken to. We smiled for visitors, and when they left, we went back to walking on eggshells.

On Sundays, the Thompsons put us in matching clothes and marched us into church like trophies.

Folks would pat their backs and say, "God bless y'all for taking in those poor children."

I used to want to scream, We're not saved! We're surviving!

But children's words don't carry weight when adults are busy performing holiness.

Mr. Thompson worked construction and drank like it was a second job. When he was drunk, he'd preach about discipline — about how "spare the rod, spoil the child" was his favorite verse.

He had a belt named Justice. We knew the sound it made slicing through the air.

Sometimes, after the beatings, Mrs. Thompson would pray over us. "Lord, make these children obedient."

I used to wonder why she never prayed for God to make them kind. I learned how to disappear without leaving the room. I'd stare at the wall until it blurred. I'd hum songs in my head Mama used to sing. I'd pretend that every creak of the floorboard was her coming to get us.

But no one came.

One night, after Mr. Thompson had one too many whiskeys, he threw a plate at my brother for spilling milk. The plate shattered against the wall, and pieces cut my arm. I still have the scar — a little white line that reminds me why I don't trust people who brag about being good Christians.

We stayed with the Thompsons for almost eight years. Eight years of pretending. Eight years of calling strangers "Mama" and "Daddy."

Outside that house, I learned how to lie to survive. At school, when teachers asked how things were, I said "fine." When social workers visited, I smiled and said we were "blessed." Because if you told the truth, you paid for it later.

Mrs. Thompson used to whisper, "Snitches go back to group homes." That was enough to keep us quiet.

So we built our own language — looks, nods, signals. A squeeze of the hand meant I'm scared. Two blinks meant stay quiet. A deep breath meant we'll get through it.

There were small mercies. My older brother could draw — he'd sketch superheroes on notebook paper and slide them under my door. He'd write little captions: We always escape.

I held on to those drawings like Bible verses. They reminded me there was a world beyond those walls. When I turned sixteen, I started working at a diner after school. It was the first time I ever felt free. The smell of burgers and grease was heaven compared to the smell of control.

Mrs. Thompson hated that job because it gave me independence. She said, "You don't need money; you've got a roof."

But money meant options. Options meant escape. The first real act of rebellion I ever did was buy my own Bible. Not the one she forced on us — my Bible. One I could actually read for myself.

That's how I found God — not through their punishment, but through my private conversations with Him.

Late at night, after everyone went to bed, I'd read under the covers. I found verses about mercy and love, not fear and control. I underlined one that still carries me today:

"Whom the Son sets free is free indeed." — John 8:36

That verse taught me something the Thompsons never could — that faith isn't about submission to people, it's about surrender to truth.

When I turned eighteen, I left that house with a duffel bag and $200. Mrs. Thompson hugged me in front of the church, pretending to cry. She told everyone how proud she was of "raising such a fine young woman."

I smiled for the photos, but my eyes were dry.

Inside, I was already gone.

Freedom felt strange at first. I'd spent so long being told what to do that I didn't know who I was without orders. For a while, I drifted — couch to couch, city to city. I worked jobs, made mistakes, chased peace like it was a moving target.

But I never forgot that house. And I never forgot what it taught me.

It taught me that not everyone who says "God" knows Him. It taught me that religion without compassion is just theater. It taught me that silence can be louder than screams.

Those lessons built a kind of strength in me that no one could see yet — the quiet kind, forged in fire.

I didn't realize it then, but surviving that house prepared me for every storm that came later — even addiction. Because once you learn to survive people who claim to love you while hurting you, surviving a drug feels almost simple.

When I reunited with my siblings years later, we compared stories. Some of them had kind foster homes, but most didn't. We all carried the same ache — that feeling of being "rescued" and ruined at the same time.

One of my brothers said, "They called it love, but it was ownership."

We nodded because that was it exactly. We weren't raised; we were managed.

And when you grow up being managed, you start to believe love is supposed to hurt. That's why I stayed in bad relationships later. That's why I didn't see the red flags when people tried to control me — I thought control was care. It took years and God's patience to unlearn that lie.

I sometimes wonder what happened to the Thompsons. Whether they ever realized the damage they did behind closed doors. Part of me used to wish for revenge, but now I just pray God gave them truth. Because truth burns longer than vengeance ever could.

Every time I tell this part of my story, people ask, "Why didn't you tell someone?"

And I say, "Who was I supposed to tell? The same system that put me there?"

That's the reality of foster care nobody wants to talk about. Once they "place" you, they move on. As long as you're not dead or missing, you're considered a success story.

But I was living proof that survival isn't the same as being safe.

Looking back, I can honestly thank God for one thing — He never let their version of faith destroy mine. Somehow, His voice still reached me through all their noise.

Because when you've seen God misrepresented that bad, the real thing becomes impossible to mistake.

That's how I learned the difference between religion and relationship. Religion kept me scared; relationship kept me alive.

So when people hear my story and say, "You're still here, Yogyrl — how?" I tell them, Because God was in the cracks of my cage.

Now, when I meet young women who've been through the system, I tell them the same thing I tell myself: You don't owe your survival story to anyone who wouldn't have saved you.

You owe it to yourself to keep healing.

The Thompsons may have tried to break me, but they built my resilience by accident. Every slap, every insult, every fake prayer — it all pushed me toward the real God, the real peace, the real me.

So, no, the Thompsons weren't my family. But they were the lesson that taught me how to build one when the time came.

Family, I've learned, isn't always the people who raise you — it's the people who help you rise.

And though that house tried to bury me under its silence, my roots found the light anyway.

I'm free now. And freedom, real freedom, feels like finally being able to breathe without asking permission.

That's the kind of home I live in today — the one inside my chest, built from forgiveness, not fear.

The Thompsons never taught me love. But loving myself despite them? That's the greatest lesson I ever learned.

CHAPTER 5
Growing Up Broken & Brave

When I left the Thompsons' house at eighteen, I didn't walk out — I ran. I didn't even look back.

I had two hundred dollars, a duffel bag full of thrift-store clothes, and a heart full of anger disguised as courage. I told myself I was free, but truth be told, I didn't even know what freedom meant yet.

When you grow up under control, you mistake chaos for choice. I thought being grown meant doing whatever I wanted — staying out late, smoking, drinking, falling into arms that felt like safety but weren't. I called it "living." It was really just running.

But running was all I knew how to do.

My first apartment was a one-room hole above a laundromat. The floor creaked, the water smelled like metal, and the heater coughed more than it worked. But it was mine.

I could play music as loud as I wanted. I could leave dishes in the sink. I could cry without someone telling me to "hush before the neighbors hear."

For a while, that was enough.

I worked double shifts at the diner and still came home with just enough money for rent and ramen noodles. But I didn't care. I was out. I was free.

Freedom, though, has a way of showing you how unprepared you are.

The first man I ever fell for was named Troy. He was charming in that way dangerous men always are — soft voice, good smile, Bible verse tattooed on his forearm like proof of righteousness.

He told me he liked how strong I was. "You don't take no mess," he said. "I need a woman like that."

For the first time in my life, someone called my pain strength. I confused that for love.

At first, he was gentle. Then the words changed.
"You don't listen."
"You too loud."
"You think you better than me."

Next came the shoves, the slaps, the apologies. "You make me crazy," he'd say. "But I love you."

I stayed, because love was supposed to hurt, right? That's what I'd been taught. That's what I'd seen.

But one night, he pushed me so hard I hit the corner of a table and blacked out. When I came to, he was crying, saying, "I didn't mean it."

I looked at him and saw every foster parent, every liar, every false savior I'd ever known — and I left. Barefoot.

That was the first night I realized being brave doesn't always look strong. Sometimes, it looks like walking away bleeding.

After Troy, I made a vow to myself: no more letting people treat me like less than. But vows made in pain don't always hold up in peace.

I drifted through jobs — waitress, cashier, janitor, receptionist. I did what I had to do to stay alive. But somewhere in between those shifts, I started hardening.

I stopped trusting people. I stopped trusting myself. I built walls so thick that even love couldn't get through.

People said, "You so strong." They meant "You so guarded."

They called it independence. I called it survival.

But I wasn't just surviving — I was also observing. Watching the world. Watching people. I noticed how everybody wore masks. How the same people who looked down on addicts were addicted to attention, status, gossip, and greed.

I saw women lose themselves trying to please men. Men lose themselves trying to impress women. People lose themselves chasing everything but peace.

And I realized something: I wasn't the only broken one. I was just one of the few honest enough to admit it.

Around that time, I started hanging around a group of women from work. We'd sit in the parking lot after shifts, passing cheap wine and swapping stories about men, money, and mistakes.

One of them, Renee, was older — maybe in her forties — and she had this calm about her. She told me, "Baby, strength without softness will make you lonely."

I didn't get it then, but she was right. I was brave, but I was hard. Brave, but bitter. Brave, but still bleeding.

You can't heal if you're always in defense mode.

I tried to go to church for a while. The first Sunday I walked in, I sat in the back, nervous. I didn't know the songs. I didn't know the lingo. But when the choir sang "Amazing Grace," I broke down.

I cried so hard I couldn't stop. It was like every tear I'd held in for years was taking its turn.

After service, a woman hugged me and said, "God heard you."

That was the first time anyone had told me that God wasn't just watching me — He was listening. That moment planted a seed.

But faith doesn't erase trauma overnight. I still had anger tucked under my tongue like a blade. When life got hard, I'd snap. When people got close, I'd push them away before they could hurt me.

I was a master of pretending. I'd smile when I wanted to scream. I'd say "I'm good" when I was anything but. I'd party like I was happy and wake up empty.

For a while, I filled that emptiness with alcohol, weed, and late nights. I told myself it was fun, that I was "just living." But deep down, I knew I was avoiding something.

Avoiding the silence. Avoiding the memories. Avoiding me.

Then, at twenty-two, I got pregnant with my twins.

I remember the doctor's voice saying, "Two heartbeats." I laughed and cried at the same time. For once, life inside me made me want to live better.

I stopped drinking. Stopped partying. Started dreaming again.

For the first time, I had something to lose that wasn't just me.

My pregnancy wasn't easy, but every kick reminded me that I wasn't alone anymore. I used to talk to them while I cleaned the diner at night.

"Mama's gonna do right by you," I'd whisper. "You gon' have what I didn't."

When they were born — two beautiful baby girls — I felt purpose for the first time.

Holding them felt like redemption.

Motherhood changed me. It softened me. But it also terrified me. I was determined to be everything Mama couldn't be — but I was still healing from things I hadn't faced.

The world doesn't stop testing you just because you're trying to do right. Bills, heartbreak, loneliness — all of it still found me.

I made mistakes. I dated the wrong men. I took shortcuts trying to make ends meet. I let exhaustion drive my decisions.

But every night, I'd check on my babies sleeping and whisper, "You safe. You loved. You mine."

And that kept me going.

When people hear about my later addiction, they don't realize how many years of holding it together came before the fall. I wasn't weak. I was worn out.

I was a woman doing everything she could to keep from repeating her mama's story — and still getting pulled into the same pain she swore she'd escape.

That's what "broken but brave" really means.
It means you keep going even when you're cracked open.
It means you keep loving even when love's been used against you.
It means you fall, but you don't stay down.

There's a strength that comes from suffering that people who've never struggled can't understand. It's the kind of strength that don't need validation.

When you've slept on floors, survived fists, faced demons, and still got up in the morning to go to work — you don't need applause.

You just need a moment to breathe.

That's what I wanted most back then — just one peaceful breath.

Sometimes I think about how brave we all are, even when we don't feel like it.

The single mama walking to work with her baby in the stroller — brave. The ex-addict saying "no" one more time — brave. The child standing up to the same kind of abuse I faced — brave.

We don't get medals for it, but God keeps score.

I didn't know it yet, but all those battles — the foster care, the beatings, the heartbreak, the survival — were training me for the hardest test I'd ever face.

The day my twins were taken from me by death.

But that part of the story comes later.

For now, this chapter ends with me standing on the edge of womanhood — tired but hopeful, fragile but fearless.

Broken, yes. But brave enough to keep living. Brave enough to believe that maybe, just maybe, God hadn't given up on me yet.

These hands have histories: the handshakes that demanded respect, the fists you unclenched to choose peace, the palms that held children close, the fingers that signed contracts and opened doors. Yet their story is also present, written fresh each time they find me. In your hands, I do not just feel safety—I feel freedom. I feel the permission to let go, to trust, to rest.

And still, your hands are not only protection or passion—they are vision. With them, you build futures. You plant seeds, both literal and figurative, and tend them. You mend what is broken, not just in wood or wire, but in hearts. You remind me that creation is a form of love, and your hands are always creating—beauty, stability, tenderness, pleasure.

I sometimes trace the lines of your palms and wonder what the world sees when you pass by. Do they notice the artistry of those hands, or only their strength? Do they imagine the gentleness that hides in the grip? I know the secret: your hands are not only power—they are prayer. Each caress feels like something offered, not taken. Each embrace is a benediction, a blessing in flesh and bone.

So let me say it plain: My Love, your hands are holy to me. They are the first sanctuary I run to and the last place I want to leave. They have built a home for my heart, and they continue to protect and caress it, day after day, night after night.

CHAPTER 6
The Twins, The Streets & The Pipe

The night I lost my twins, the world went silent.

No sirens, no heartbeat, no sound loud enough to match the crack inside my chest. One moment I was their mama—the next I was just a woman standing in the hallway of a hospital trying to remember how to breathe. The doctor's lips were moving, but all I heard was the hum of the fluorescent lights above me. When grief hits that deep, sound stops meaning anything.

After the funeral I didn't go home; home didn't exist anymore. Their toys were still there. Their clothes still smelled like baby lotion. I'd sit in their room and talk to them like they could hear me, then I'd stare out the window until sunrise. People said time heals everything. Time didn't heal me—it only gave the pain new places to hide.

I tried to keep working. Tried to keep smiling when customers said, "How are the twins?" and I'd answer, "They're fine," because explaining was too heavy. Every word felt like lifting a boulder.

When the bills stacked up and the walls started closing in, I started walking. Long walks through the city, sometimes until my legs gave out. I saw other people out there—faces worn, eyes hollow—each of them trying to forget something. They weren't evil. They were just tired like me.

That's how the streets found me. Or maybe I found them.

People like to make addiction sound like a choice. But when your heart's been blown apart and you're still expected to show up for life, anything that promises silence starts looking like salvation.

I won't glorify it, and I won't detail it, but I will tell the truth: grief can become a drug long before you ever touch one. I was already addicted—to numbness, to forgetting, to not feeling that empty space where my babies should have been.

For a while, the streets gave me a kind of fellowship. Other lost ones, all of us pretending we weren't. We shared laughter that never reached our eyes. We shared stories that always ended with "but I'm okay now," even when we weren't.

Then came the whisper. Not from the streets, but from somewhere deeper.

"This isn't who you are."

At first I ignored it. But the whisper didn't stop. It came when I was alone. It came when I tried to sleep. It came every time I looked in a mirror and saw a woman I didn't recognize.

That whisper was God calling me back through the noise.

One morning, after another sleepless night, I caught my own reflection and said out loud, "You still alive. You still somebody's child. Get up."

I fell to my knees on that cold floor and cried until my throat burned. I didn't know how to pray, so I just talked. "God, if You still want me, take me out of this. Please."

I didn't feel lightning or angels. But I did feel peace slide in like quiet water. That was the beginning of clean.

Getting clean wasn't a straight road. It was a crawl. Some days I stood tall; some days I shook. But every day, I talked to God. I told Him everything—the guilt, the shame, the loneliness. And He listened. I could feel it. That's how I knew I wasn't beyond saving.

People from my past looked shocked when they saw me start to glow again. They'd ask, "You still in that life?" and I'd smile and say, "No, I'm in my life now."

Eight years later, I'm still in it.

Now, when I walk past the same streets that once held me hostage, I pray for the people still standing there. Not from pity—from understanding. I know what it's like to want peace so bad you'll take poison that pretends to be it.

But I also know what it's like to come back.

The twins are gone, but they're not lost. I carry them with me in every testimony, in every person who hears my story and decides to fight one more day. Their lives birthed my purpose.

When people ask how I survived, I tell them: Grief broke me, but God rebuilt me.

The streets showed me darkness, but the same God who let me walk through it was already waiting at the end with light.

That's the truth I live now. You can be shattered and still shine. You can lose everything and still find yourself. You can walk through fire and come out gold.

CHAPTER 7
God Found Me Before I Found Him

People always say, "I found God."

But that's not my story. God found me.

He found me in the silence between sobs, in the nights when I thought the world would be better off without me. He found me before I ever knew how to look for Him.

When I first started trying to live clean, I didn't have a plan—just pain and prayer. I was still shaky, still full of guilt, still hearing the old voices in my head: You're not worth saving. You'll mess it up again. But every morning, before my feet hit the floor, I whispered, "Thank You." I didn't even know what I was thanking Him for—maybe just for the breath that proved I was still here.

At first, praying felt awkward. I wasn't raised in church. The Thompsons made me memorize Scripture, but they never taught me what a real conversation with God sounded like. I thought prayer had to be perfect, like poetry. Turns out, God just wanted honesty.

So I started talking to Him like He was sitting right next to me.

"God, I don't know what You see in me, but I'm trying."
"God, help me not go back."
"God, it hurts today."
"God, thank You for keeping me from myself."

And slowly, the more I talked, the more peace answered back.

I began spending my evenings walking instead of wandering. I'd walk past the same corners that used to swallow me and whisper, Thank You for getting me out. Sometimes I'd run into old faces from that life. They'd squint, trying to recognize me.

"Diamond, that you? Girl, you look different."

I'd laugh. "Yeah. God gave me a new face. You can't buy this glow."

It wasn't makeup. It was mercy.

I didn't get sober through programs or sponsors. My sponsor was the Holy Spirit. My meetings were sunrise talks with God and sunset walks with my thoughts. Don't get me wrong—AA and NA helped me see Him. But they couldn't keep me when only faith could.

See, programs teach you to count days. God taught me to count grace.

During that first year of recovery, I started writing in a notebook—just conversations between me and God. I called it Our Talks. Sometimes I'd write angry letters: "Why did You take my twins?" Sometimes grateful ones: "Thank You for waking me up clean." I didn't realize it then, but those pages were becoming the bones of this very book.

One night, while I was writing, I heard a thought whisper clear as a bell:

Tell them I never left you.

I froze. My hands shook. I knew that voice wasn't mine. It was the same calm that had pulled me out years before. I whispered back, "I'll tell them, Lord. I'll tell them all."

That was the night I decided to stop hiding my story.

The first time I stood up and gave my testimony at a women's meeting, my knees knocked so bad I thought I'd fall. I looked around the room—church ladies, businesswomen, young girls fresh out of jail—and said, "I don't have a polished story. I just have proof."

Then I told them: "I smoked crack. So what? I don't anymore. And the same God who loved me in my mess loves you in yours."

When I finished, the room was quiet for a long time. Then a woman in the back started clapping through her tears. "Thank you," she said. "I thought I was the only one."

That's when I realized: shame can't survive truth spoken out loud.

After that, doors started opening. Small churches asked me to share. Women stopped me in grocery stores saying, "Aren't you the lady who talks about getting free?" I didn't plan a ministry, but God built one out of my brokenness.

He even sent me mentors—real ones. Not perfect saints, but healed women who knew what rock bottom felt like. They didn't judge me for my past; they trained me for my purpose. One of them, Sister Joyce, told me, "Baby, don't let people worship your testimony and forget the Testifier." That line changed everything.

I stopped talking so much about the drugs and started talking more about deliverance.

It wasn't all smooth. Some folks from my past still called me "the crackhead that found religion." Others tried to test my peace—bringing gossip, old temptations, and reminders of who I used to be.

But the closer I walked with God, the quieter their noise got. He didn't just remove the craving from my body; He removed the chaos from my mind. He cleaned house.

I learned to recognize His voice—the gentle nudge that said, Don't answer that call, or Go left, not right. Sometimes it sounded like intuition; sometimes like silence. But I trusted it.

Because when God finds you, He keeps guiding you.

One afternoon, during my second year clean, I visited the cemetery where my twins are buried. I brought flowers—yellow, their favorite color. I sat between their headstones and said, "I'm okay now. Mama's doing better." The wind picked up, soft but sure, and I felt warmth on my face though the sun was behind clouds. I smiled. "I know," I whispered. "I know You're here."

Grief still visits me, but now it brings peace with it. The pain turned into purpose. God turned mourning into ministry.

I started volunteering at shelters and transitional homes. The first time I told a group of women my story, one of them shouted, "You talk like you still remember how it feels."
I said, "I do. That's why I can help you out of it."

See, healing isn't forgetting; it's remembering without staying stuck.

Every woman I met reminded me of a piece of myself—the scared girl, the angry teen, the exhausted mama. I'd look into their eyes and think, That was me. And they'd look back at me like, Maybe that can be me someday.

That's how God works: He recycles pain into purpose.

I didn't realize how far I'd come until one day I caught my reflection again—this time in a store window. I stopped and said, "You look like peace." I meant it.

No makeup, no filter, just peace. The old me chased validation. The new me carries it.

The old me begged people to understand. The new me doesn't need approval to be grateful.

People sometimes ask, "Yogyrl, how do you stay clean without meetings?"
And I tell them, "I have a meeting every morning—with God."

No minutes, no coffee cups, no folding chairs— just me and Him and a new sunrise. I open my window, breathe deep, and say, "Thank You for another chance." That's recovery.

The Bible says, "The Lord is close to the brokenhearted and saves those who are crushed in spirit." (Psalm 34:18). I used to think "brokenhearted" meant weak. Now I know it means available. When your heart's cracked wide open, there's finally room for God to get in.

He got in. And He never left.

Sometimes, late at night, I think about how far I've come—from that scared little girl watching her mama fade, to the foster child learning fear, to the woman who lost everything and still stood back up.

I don't glamorize the struggle, but I do honor it. Because without it, I wouldn't have found faith that deep.

Or maybe faith wouldn't have found me.

God met me on the floor of my worst day and walked me into the sunrise of my best. I didn't earn it; I just accepted it. That's grace—undeserved, unstoppable, and unexplainable.

So when people say, "You must really love God," I smile and say, "He loved me first."

CHAPTER 8
Clean Don't Mean Quiet

People act like getting clean means you're supposed to disappear.

Like the minute you stop using, you're supposed to become soft, sweet, and silent—some grateful little church mouse whispering, "Thank You for saving me."

Nah. I'm grateful, but I'm not quiet.

Clean don't mean quiet. Clean means clear. Clear about who I am. Clear about what I won't allow. Clear about the God who carried me out and the peace I refuse to give back.

When I first started walking in sobriety, folks didn't know how to handle me. They liked the broken version of me better—the one who needed favors, borrowed money, and said sorry for existing. They could pity her. They could feel superior.

But this new me? The one who says no without guilt? The one who knows her worth? She made people uncomfortable.

I used to shrink myself just to keep friends. I used to explain every boundary like it was a court case. Now I just say, "Because I said so."

That's what healing does—it turns "please like me" into "please leave me if you have to."

The hardest part wasn't quitting drugs; it was quitting the need to be understood.

People love the idea of redemption stories until they realize redemption comes with a backbone. When I started speaking up, some folks called it attitude. I call it confidence baptized in truth.

They'd say, "You so defensive."

I'd say, "No, I'm just done letting people write lies about my life."

I don't defend my past anymore. I define it.

For years, people tried to keep me trapped in the same sentence: Yogyrl, the addict.

But that's not my name. My name means precious, rare, chosen.

So when I walk into a room now, I carry myself like someone God hand-delivered from hell and told, "Speak." Because that's exactly what He did.

Sometimes after church, people come up whispering, "You don't have to tell all your business like that."

And I smile and say, "You don't have to listen."

The truth offends those still protecting lies.

See, silence is how shame survives. That's why I talk loud. Not for attention—but for liberation. Every time I open my mouth, another woman realizes she's not crazy, not dirty, not alone.

That's ministry to me—turning my scars into sound.

Being clean taught me how to read spirits, not faces. I can tell when someone's cheering for me and when they're just waiting for me to fall.

You can feel the difference.

The cheerleaders pray for you; the watchers pray on you.

So I started trimming my circle. No announcement, no drama—just quiet exits. I used to chase people who drained me; now I guard my energy like it's sacred currency. Because it is.

The first year I got clean, I apologized to everybody.

"I'm sorry for what I said."

"I'm sorry for what I did."

Half of them didn't even remember. The other half used it to keep me small.

Now my apologies come with balance. If I wronged you, I'll own it. But if you only remember my sin and not your cruelty, that's your confession to make, not mine.

Forgiveness doesn't mean foolishness.

I also learned that peace needs maintenance. You can't just get free and assume freedom will babysit itself. I pray daily, I rest on purpose, and I keep reminders around me of where I came from—photos of my twins, my old notebook, a candle that says "Whole."

Those things keep me grounded. Because humility isn't saying you're nothing; it's remembering Who rescued you.

When I speak at recovery centers now, I tell the women, "Don't trade your silence for acceptance." I see them nodding, tears in their eyes, and I know they get it. The world wants us ashamed. But shame doesn't serve God; truth does.

Some of them whisper after, "Aren't you scared people will judge you?"
And I say, "They already did. I survived it."

Once you've been judged by everyone and still forgiven by God, human opinions start sounding small.

There was a time when gossip about me could ruin my whole week. Now it can't ruin my coffee. I sip slow and smile. Because I know gossip dies when the truth walks in.

One day, a woman who used to party with me saw me in the store and said, "Girl, you acting brand-new."
I laughed. "I am brand-new. The old model broke."

She didn't know whether to hug me or hate me. That's not my business.

Another thing I learned: some people only loved the version of me they could rescue. The minute I didn't need saving, they disappeared.

At first that hurt. Then God showed me—it wasn't rejection, it was release. They were never assigned to my healed life. They were only part of my survival season.

That revelation set me free.

Because every upgrade requires off-loading old luggage.

Being outspoken doesn't mean I'm angry; it means I'm alive. I use my voice because so many women never got the chance. Some are still in graves of guilt, buried by other people's opinions. I dig with words until they breathe again.

And when critics say, "You too real," I remind them: Jesus was too real for the Pharisees too.

I still have moments of quiet, but it's a peaceful quiet, not the scared kind. The scared kind hides; the peaceful kind heals.

Now when I'm silent, it's because I'm listening—to God, to my body, to my boundaries. My silence is chosen, not stolen.

Sometimes people ask, "Yogyrl, how do you deal with triggers?"

I tell them, "By telling the truth faster than the lie can grow."

When pain whispers, You're still that same girl, I answer, "Maybe, but she's got armor now."

When temptation says, One hit won't hurt, I say, "One prayer will help."

When guilt says, *Nobody believes you changed,* I say, "God saw it first."

That's how I fight—word for Word.

There's a verse that became my anthem:

"Let the redeemed of the Lord say so." — Psalm 107:2

It doesn't say whisper so. It says say so. Out loud. Bold. Unashamed.

Because testimony loses power when it stays private.

Now, eight years free, I don't just speak in churches. I talk in schools, jails, shelters, parks— anywhere ears are open. Some people come expecting pity stories. They leave with purpose stories.

I tell them, "Don't call yourself an addict forever if God already calls you free."
Language is power. Speak the name you're growing into, not the one you outgrew.

Being clean gave me clarity, but speaking truth gave me strength. They work together. You can't stay clean if you stay silent about the mess that almost killed you.

So I talk. Loud. Honest. Unapologetic.
Because every word is another chain breaking—mine and somebody else's.

People sometimes say, "Girl, you talk like you got nothing to lose."
I smile and say, "I already lost everything once. That's why I speak like everything I say might save someone."

Clean doesn't mean quiet. It means courageous. It means conscious. It means called.

And when God calls, you answer—sometimes with tears, sometimes with testimony, but never with silence.

CHAPTER 9
Let Me Reintroduce Myself

For most of my life, people introduced me before I could open my mouth.

"Yogyrl — the addict."

"Yogyrl — the one who lost her twins and they got killed."

"Yogyrl — the foster kid."

"Yogyrl – the molestation victim."

So let me set the record straight. I am not who you remember. Allow me to reintroduce myself.

I'm Yogyrl Diamond — child of God, mother, survivor, business-owner, and living proof that resurrection isn't just for Easter Sunday.

When people see me now, they see confidence. They see calm. What they don't see are the nights I built this peace out of pieces, brick by prayer, tear by tear. They don't see the empty refrigerator, the eviction notice, the panic attacks that tried to pull me back under.

They only see the glow. And that's fine. I earned every watt of this light.

After I got steady, I promised myself two things: Never hide again. Never hand my power back to other people's opinions.

So I started small — a side hustle selling handmade candles with scriptures on the labels. "Faith Lights," I called them. Each one carried a verse that had carried me. I sold them from my trunk at first, then online, then in boutiques. Within a year, it turned into a business.

The same hands that once trembled from withdrawal now poured wax, tied ribbons, and mailed packages with prayers tucked inside.

Every order felt like God saying, See? I can turn ashes into aroma.

My daughter helped me set up a website. Watching her type "Founder — Yogyrl Diamond" almost made me cry. She doesn't remember the darkest years; she just sees her mama hustling legally, smiling genuinely, loving loudly.

That's the beauty of redemption — your children get to know the healed version of you.

But success brought its own tests. Some folks couldn't handle my shine.

Who she think she is now?" they'd whisper.

I think I'm free. That's who.

I stopped dimming my light just because their eyes still prefer darkness.

See, humility isn't pretending you're still broken; it's giving God credit for putting you back together.

My business wasn't the only thing God restored. He restored relationships — the healthy kind. My siblings and I talk again, not out of obligation but out of choice.

We've all learned to say, "I love you," without adding, "even though we hurt each other."

We survived hell, and now we choose heaven daily — right here on Earth, in forgiveness.

At family gatherings, someone always jokes, "Don't let Yogyrl get the mic, she'll start preaching."

And I laugh because it's true. But it's not preaching; it's gratitude with a voice.

People often ask, "When did you finally believe you were different?"

It happened the day I stopped reacting to disrespect. Someone tried to drag me back into an old argument.

Instead of snapping, I smiled and said, "I don't live there anymore." That sentence felt like graduation.

Because peace, once you have it, becomes a home you refuse to rent out to chaos.

I've learned to celebrate myself without apology. Birthdays used to depress me — another year of surviving. Now they excite me — another year of purpose. On my last birthday, I wrote this in my journal:

Dear God, thank You for not letting the devil have the final edit on my story.

That's my reintroduction in one line.

I started mentoring younger women coming out of recovery programs. Some just need a ride to work. Some need someone to talk to who won't clutch pearls at their truth. I tell them, "I'm not your counselor, I'm your evidence."

One of them said, "Miss Diamond, you make me believe I can start over too."

I said, "Baby, don't just start over — start right."

Because starting over without healing just makes a new version of the same pain.

I've also reintroduced myself to the mirror. For years, I couldn't look too long. Now I do daily check-ins:

"How we feeling?"

"What we grateful for?"

"Who we forgiving today?"

Sometimes the answer is myself. Healing isn't linear. Some mornings I still wake up heavy. But now I know what to do with the weight — hand it to God before breakfast.

Old friends who still live half-truths sometimes call me "too holy."

I tell them, "I'm not holy; I'm whole."

There's a difference. Holiness tries to impress people. Wholeness just impresses peace.

Reintroducing myself meant retiring guilt as my identity.

Guilt says, "You owe the world proof you've changed."

Grace says, "You owe God thanks for changing you."

I choose grace. So when people gossip, I let them. When they test me, I pray for them. When they doubt me, I remind myself — faith doesn't need witnesses.

These days, my schedule is full — business orders, speaking invites, mentoring calls—but my spirit is light. I tithe time now — an hour each morning just to be still. Coffee, candle, Scripture. That's my boardroom meeting with Heaven.

That's where new ideas come from. God gives me downloads like, Write the next book, Start the podcast, Help that woman you met yesterday. I used to doubt my intuition. Now I recognize it as instruction.

Reintroduction also means redefining beauty. I used to think beauty meant hiding scars. Now I show them. Not because I'm proud of pain, but because proof helps somebody else believe in healing.

Every line on my face tells a story: the foster home, the streets, the comeback. My reflection doesn't shame me anymore; it introduces me.

"Hi, I'm Yogyrl Diamond. Unbreakable, unstoppable, and unashamed."

I can't tell you life suddenly became easy. Bills still come. People still betray. The world still spins crazy. But the difference now is that my foundation doesn't crack when life shakes.

I built it on truth, not image. On faith, not fear. On purpose, not pain.

Sometimes, when I'm on stage speaking, I catch sight of a woman in the back wiping tears. I see myself in her.

So I stop mid-sentence and say, "Sis, you can start again right now. You don't have to wait for permission."

That's what this whole chapter is—a permission slip. So if you've ever met the old me, allow me to reintroduce myself:

I'm the woman who outlived the rumor. I'm the mother who still mothers even when heaven holds her children. I'm the believer who prays in plain English. I'm the businesswoman who built profit out of pain. I'm the friend who listens without judging. I'm the warrior who sleeps in peace.

And I'm not done yet. God's still editing my sequel.

Reintroduction isn't about forgetting your past. It's about refusing to let your past narrate your present. Every time I tell my story, I close another chapter of shame and open another page of grace.

So, world, now that you know me — not the gossip, not the ghost, not the girl who almost gave up — I hope you're ready for the woman who walked out of fire carrying a microphone.

My name is Yogyrl Diamond. Remember it, respect it, and repeat it only if you're ready to spell freedom correctly.

CHAPTER 10
I'm Not Your Victim, I'm Your Reminder

When people look at me now, they still tilt their heads the same way they did back then—half curiosity, half disbelief. Like they're trying to figure out how somebody who went through that much can still smile.

Here's the answer: I stopped being a victim the day I stopped letting shame narrate my story.

I used to hate running into people who "knew me when." You know the type—mouth full of gossip, heart half-full of grace.

They'd start a sentence with, "I remember when you ..."

And I'd cut them off with, "Yeah, and I remember when God flipped it."

Because if you're going to bring up my past, you better be ready to talk about my resurrection.

The truth is, most of the people who try to define me by my lowest point are terrified of what my comeback says about their comfort. My survival exposes their stagnation. My faith exposes their fake. My freedom reminds them they could change too—but they'd rather criticize than confront themselves.

That's why I say I'm not your victim—I'm your reminder.

Every time you see me winning, it's proof that excuses don't work when grace shows up.

Some folks wear victimhood like jewelry—they love the sympathy it buys. Not me. I traded pity for purpose. I don't want your tears; I want your transformation.

If my story makes you uncomfortable, good. That means the truth hit a nerve. And nerves only hurt where healing still needs to happen.

I remember the first time someone called me a "miracle." We were at a women's conference.

A lady came up crying, saying, "You give me hope."

I hugged her and whispered, "That's what miracles do—they multiply."

Because a miracle isn't just a moment; it's a message that keeps spreading. But miracles also make people mad. When they can't explain how you got out, they start trying to discredit how you did it.

"Oh, she just got lucky."

"Oh, she found religion."

No, baby—I found redemption. The world wants survivors to stay silent so it can stay comfortable. It loves a comeback story as long as you tell it politely. But I don't owe anyone politeness for pain I paid full price for.

So yes, I speak blunt. Yes, I call out hypocrisy. Yes, I quote Scripture and street slang in the same breath. Because that's me—holy and hood, grace and grit, healed but still human.

People ask, "Don't you ever get tired of telling your story?"

Sometimes I do. But then I remember the women who still can't tell theirs. The ones sitting in shame, thinking they're the only ones. The ones whose families still call them junkies instead of fighters. For them, I keep talking. My voice is my weapon, my witness, and my worship.

Every "so what?" I say is another chain snapping somewhere I can't even see.

I've learned that forgiveness isn't approval—it's release. I forgave the Thompsons. I forgave the man who hit me. I even forgave the people who still whisper about me after church. Not because they deserve it, but because I deserve peace.

Forgiveness is like spring-cleaning for the soul— you throw out what smells like bitterness so joy has room to move in.

Nowadays, when someone tries to "remind" me of my past, I smile. You can't use what I already testified about as a weapon. Confession disarms gossip. That's why the devil hates honesty—truth takes away his job description.

I still have scars—on my body, in my memory— but I've stopped hiding them. They're not shame marks; they're survival stamps.

Every one says, "God kept me when people counted me out."

When I walk into a room now, I don't enter like a tragedy. I enter like evidence. Evidence that mercy is still hiring, that grace still works overtime, and that resurrection is still a daily event.

Sometimes I think about my twins and wonder what they'd say if they could see me now.

I imagine them smiling and saying, "Mama, you did it."

I whisper back, "We did."

Because their short lives planted the seed that grew into my purpose. Their memory is my ministry. Their absence became the space where God built my voice.

I also think about Mama.
If she were alive, I'd tell her, "You didn't die in vain. I broke the cycle."

All her pain became prophecy. She couldn't see the harvest, but she planted the faith. Now I'm living in the field she watered with her tears.

The older I get, the more I realize victory isn't loud—it's consistent. It's getting up every morning and choosing peace instead of revenge, prayer instead of pity, gratitude instead of gossip. That's the real flex.

People expect fireworks after freedom. What they don't expect is how normal it feels to finally be stable. How holy "boring" can be when drama used to be your drug. Peace used to scare me because it was quiet; now I guard it like treasure.

There's one scripture that sums up my whole life:

"What you meant for evil, God turned for good." — Genesis 50:20

That's the tattoo on my heart. Everything that tried to kill me ended up confirming my calling. That's how divine reversal works.

So to everyone who ever counted me out—thank you. You became my motivation playlist.

Sometimes I get messages online from people saying, "You're too confident for someone with your past."

I reply, "Confidence isn't arrogance—it's gratitude in motion."

I walk tall because I know what it's like to crawl. I speak boldly because silence almost buried me. And I love loudly because hate already had enough airtime.

If you're reading this thinking you're too far gone, let me remind you: I was, too. And look at me now.

I'm not your victim—I'm your reminder that grace doesn't expire. You don't have to be perfect to be powerful. You don't have to be spotless to be chosen. You just have to be willing.

God specializes in "used-to-be" people. I used to be lost, used to be high, used to be hopeless—now I'm used by Him. That's the glow you see.

So the next time someone says, "Weren't you the one who...?"

You tell them, "Yep—and God was the One who wasn't finished."

Because as long as you're breathing, you're becoming.

I'm not the poster child for addiction. I'm the billboard for redemption.

Let me leave you with this: Every survivor is somebody's reminder. Remind the world that healing exists. Remind the system that compassion works. Remind the next woman that her story's not over.

That's my mission now. Not to erase the pain—but to prove it didn't win.

I'm not your victim. I'm your reminder.

And every time I speak, heaven echoes, "So what?"

CHAPTER 11
Stating The Obvious

Let's stop pretending only some addictions count. If you keep doing something that hurts you or the people around you, and you can't — or won't — stop, that's addiction.

Whether it's a needle, a shopping cart, a lighter, a secret, or a lie, the effect is the same: it numbs what needs healing. I wrote this book for anyone who's tired of trying to be normal.

For anyone who sits alone, promising "just one more time."

For anyone who hides mess behind closed doors and calls it survival. If that's you, keep reading—because you don't have to hide anymore.

Nicotine — The Slow Thief

Cigarettes, cigars, vapes — they don't calm you; they claim you. They whisper that you're relaxing, but what you're really doing is buying back your own breath ten minutes at a time. I know people who can't pray or drive or even think without lighting up first.

They say, "It's my one vice."

But vice is just another word for chain.

You want to quit? Start with the next one. Wait fifteen minutes longer than usual. Do it again tomorrow. Each small delay is a protest against your own destruction.

And when you slip — and you will — don't light the next one out of guilt. Guilt is expensive smoke.

Call 1-800-QUIT-NOW. Somebody there will remind you that lungs were made for air, not fire.

Alcohol — The Legal Escape

Alcohol is the oldest trick the devil ever bottled. It starts with laughter and ends with forgetting.

People don't drink to celebrate; they drink to silence the noise of what they refuse to face.

If you can't imagine joy without a drink in your hand, you've already traded joy for anesthesia.

Try three days sober. See what your mind says when the buzz is gone.

If your hands shake or your heart races, that's your body begging for help — not more liquor.

Hospitals don't judge withdrawal; they treat it. So call **SAMHSA 1-800-662-HELP** or walk into any emergency room and say, "I think I'm in trouble." That sentence could save your life.

Weed — The "It's Just Weed" Lie

I used to laugh at folks calling marijuana addictive — until I met people who couldn't go to work, church, or sleep without it.

Addiction doesn't care if your drug is legal, herbal, or home-grown. If you need it to feel okay, you're no longer free.

Weed dulls edges, but edges are what keep us sharp enough to grow.

Take a weekend off. Notice how time slows down.

Notice what thoughts come up that you've been hiding under smoke. That's where the healing is waiting.

Cocaine and Crack — The Rush That Robs

These two are cousins — one wears diamonds, one wears dust — but they both lead to the same grave. I know because I lived it.

They trick you into thinking you're powerful, even as they drain the power right out of you. The high lasts seconds; the shame lasts days.

Throw away every pipe, straw, and number tonight. You don't need "one more." You need a mirror and a decision.

Find a meeting. Find a detox. Find a reason bigger than the craving.

And when people call you a "crackhead," remember: that label says more about their ignorance than your destiny.

Call Cocaine Anonymous 1-800-347-8998 or **SAMHSA 1-800-662-HELP.** Freedom's still free—you just have to ask for it.

Meth — The False Fire

Methamphetamine doesn't just steal—it rewires. It burns joy to keep you awake for days, then leaves you hollow for weeks. The mirror becomes your enemy, your thoughts your jailer.

I've watched faces age ten years in one season, teeth crumble, hope disappear. If that's you, don't despair. Your brain can heal; it just needs time and mercy.

Start with sleep. Real sleep. Eat fruit. Drink water. Let sunlight hit your skin.

When the paranoia whispers, "They're after you," answer out loud, "No—they're praying for me."

Then call for help before that whisper becomes a scream. **1-800-662-HELP** or **crystalmeth.org** will take your call day or night.

Heroin, Fentanyl, and Opioids — The Slow Goodbye

No drug kills quieter than opioids. You nod off today, never wake up tomorrow. But I've also seen miracles in rehab rooms — men and women who came back from literal death. They didn't do it alone.

If you're using, please don't quit cold turkey. Your body's chemistry is hostage now; you need medical release. Ask about Suboxone, Methadone, or Buprenorphine—they're not replacements, they're bridges.

Carry Narcan. Teach your friends how to use it. If anyone mocks you, tell them you'd rather be prepared than buried.

Never Use Alone 1-800-484-3731. They'll stay on the line till you're safe. You matter too much to overdose in silence.

Hallucinogens and Club Drugs — The Open Door

PCP, LSD, ecstasy, mushrooms—they promise enlightenment but often deliver psychosis. You think you're exploring your mind, but you're opening doors trauma walks right through.

I've met people who never fully came back from a single trip.

If you've started hearing or seeing what isn't real, you are not possessed—you're injured. And injuries heal with treatment, not shame.

Call **988** or walk into any ER. Say, "I took something and I'm scared." That's courage, not weakness.

Lean, Pills, and Prescriptions

"Doctor gave it to me" is not an excuse — it's an alarm.

Codeine, Xanax, Percocet—comfort wrapped in cotton. You start taking them for pain and keep taking them to avoid feeling anything.

Tell your doctor. Don't hide. Dispose of extras at a pharmacy drop-box. If you bought them off the street, stop now — half of what's sold as "Percs" is fentanyl in disguise.

Text HELP to 55753 (Partnership to End Addiction) or call **1-800-662-HELP.**

Huffing — The Silent Killer

If you inhale anything not meant for lungs—paint, gas, aerosol—you're gambling with oxygen.

One breath too long, your brain starves and never wakes up.

If someone passes out, call **911** immediately, then **Poison Control 1-800-222-1222.**

And if you survived a close call, please don't chalk it up to luck. That was grace. Use it.

Mixing Anything

Every addict thinks they've found the right cocktail. Until the cocktail finds their funeral.

Alcohol with pills, coke with weed, lean with meth—each mix doubles the odds of death.

If you've been mixing, go to the ER and say, *"I'm withdrawing from multiple substances."* That sentence can reset your life.

Hoarding and Living in Squalor — When Clutter Becomes a Cage

Let's talk about the kind of addiction no one posts online. The piles, the bags, the smell, the shame.

Hoarding is grief that never got to cry. Every object is a memory you can't process, so you keep it. Soon the stuff owns the space—and you disappear beneath it.

You are not lazy. You are overwhelmed.
Start with one small, safe corner. Clean it like it's sacred. Light a candle. Thank God for that one visible square of floor. Then tomorrow, make it two.

If you can't start alone, call **1-617-973-5801 (International OCD Foundation)** or **1-800-662-HELP** for therapy referrals. There's no judgment, only help.
Your home can breathe again, and so can you.

Shopping and Spending — The Pretty Addiction

Nobody wants to admit this one because it hides behind bags with logos. But spending is a drug too.

The hit is that swipe; the crash is the statement. You buy things to feel powerful, to feel new, to feel seen—and for a minute, it works. Then guilt shows up wearing a due date.

Freeze your cards. Tell a friend to hold them for thirty days. Unsubscribe from "flash sale" emails.

When you want to buy, write instead. "What am I trying to fix with this purchase?" Half the time it's loneliness wearing perfume.

Debtors Anonymous 1-800-421-2383 and **NFCC 1-800-388-2227** can teach you how to get free without losing everything.

Addicted to Chaos and Conflict

Some people aren't hooked on a drug—they're hooked on drama. If a day passes without a fight, a rumor, or a crisis, they get itchy. They stir the pot just to hear the boil.

You might not realize it, but chaos is a drug too. It floods your body with adrenaline and convinces you that movement equals meaning. But all it does is keep you spinning while your peace collects dust in the corner.

If you can't stand quiet, that's your first clue that silence is what you need most. Turn off the phone for one hour. Don't text, don't scroll, don't gossip. Breathe. You'll shake like a detoxing soul—but you'll live.

Get help:

- **NAMI 1-800-950-NAMI (6264)** — free counseling referrals.

- Faith-based programs on boundaries and emotional regulation.

Remember: *Stillness isn't boredom—it's balance.*

Addicted to Being the Hero

You're the rescuer, the fixer, the one who always "has it." You pay other people's bills, solve their messes, answer their 3 a.m. calls, even when your own life is falling apart. And secretly, you resent them for it.

That's not love — that's control dressed in kindness. You've mistaken usefulness for worthiness. You feel needed, not loved.

Here's the truth: God didn't make you the savior. He already sent One. Your job is to help without hijacking someone else's growth.

Start saying "no" with peace instead of guilt. Let other people fail and figure it out. That's how they learn what grace feels like, too.

Call Co-Dependents Anonymous 1-888-444-2359 or visit coda.org. They'll teach you the hardest sentence you'll ever speak: *"My life matters, too."*

Addicted to Pushing Away Love

Some of you are experts at sabotage. You meet someone kind, someone safe — and instantly you look for proof they'll hurt you. So you test them. You ghost them. You insult the ones who treat you right while clinging to the ones who treat you wrong.

You're not evil. You're scared. Abandonment trained you to expect pain, so you start the breakup before they can.

Stop confusing rejection with protection. Let someone love you long enough for the panic to pass.

And when your mind screams, "They'll leave!" answer, "Maybe — but until then, I'll enjoy being seen."

Help: Therapy via NAMI 1-800-950-NAMI or online trauma specialists. Healing attachment isn't weakness — it's warfare.

Addicted to Pain and Victimhood

Some people don't want healing — they want sympathy. Pain becomes their identity. They introduce themselves by their scars, not their stories.

I say this with love: stop making suffering your brand. Yes, you were hurt. But if you keep rehearsing it, you'll never release it. You don't owe your trauma lifetime rent in your heart.

Let the wound close. You can still tell your story—just tell it from the healed place, not the hurting one. God can't fill hands that won't let go.

Get help: Trauma-informed therapy, local support groups, or church-based recovery circles.

Addicted to Hoarding Pain and Guilt

Some people collect regret like antiques. They replay the same mistakes every night before bed, polishing shame until it shines. But guilt is useless once it's confessed. It only poisons if you keep drinking it.

Forgive yourself the way God already has. If He isn't holding it against you, why are you? Lay it down. Walk free.

Addicted to Fear

Fear is a liar with a microphone. It tells you, "Don't try — don't change — don't hope."

Every time you believe it, you worship it.

Do it scared anyway. Pick up the phone. Apply for the job. Walk into the meeting. Tell the truth. Courage isn't the absence of fear — it's motion in spite of it.

Help: 988 if fear turns into panic or hopelessness.

Addicted to Despair and Hopelessness

Depression can become a comfort zone. You start thinking sadness is safer than disappointment. But darkness isn't home—it's just familiar.

Move your body. Eat. Shower. Step outside. Then call **988** or text **HELLO** to **741741.** Hope answers faster than you think.

Addicted to Isolation

You say, "I like being alone," but you're really afraid of being seen.

You've mistaken solitude for safety, but healing happens in community. Find one person who listens without fixing. That's where trust begins again.

Help: Local churches, online recovery ommunities, or peer-support programs through **SAMHSA 1-800-662-HELP.**

Addicted to Perfection

You call it "high standards." God calls it bondage." Perfectionism isn't excellence — it's fear of being unlovable unless you perform. Relax. You were worthy before you produced anything.

Give yourself permission to be human. Progress is holiness in motion.

If You're Supporting Someone Broken

Love them, but stop rescuing them from themselves. Boundaries are holy.

Say, "I'll help you get help," not "I'll help you hide."

Pray more than you preach. Remember — addiction hates accountability but thrives in secrecy.

Universal Help Line Directory

Struggle	Helpline / Resource
ance Use & Detox	ISA 1-800-662-HELP (435
le / Self-Harm / Crisis	r text **HOME → 741741**
al Health / Depression	I **1-800-950-NAMI (6264)**
Smoking / Vaping	**-QUIT-NOW**
Jose / Use Alone	r Use Alone **1-800-484-3**7
estic Violence	**-799-SAFE (7233)**
al Assault	**-656-HOPE (4673)**
/ Street Exit	**-905-1522**
Jing / OCD Support	**-973-5801 (IOCDF)**
/ Shopping Addiction	**-421-2383 (Debtors Anoi**
pendency / Hero Addiction	**-444-2359 (CoDA)**
Jling	**-222-5542 (Gamblers An**
ddiction	**-477-8191 (SAA)**

Struggle	Helpline / Resource
Text Line (alt)	**HELLO → 741741**

If you're outside the U.S., search "mental-health helpline + [your country]." Someone is always awake somewhere, waiting to help.

Final Word In This Direction On This Shit

Addiction isn't a death sentence; it's a detour. You can always turn around. Truth breaks denial. Help breaks habit. Grace breaks chains.

Tell the truth — to yourself, to God, to someone safe. Ask for help before it kills you. Let grace do the rest.

You don't have to die to start over. You just have to stop pretending you can't. And when somebody asks how you made it, tell them plainly:

"Because I finally wanted to live more than I wanted to escape."

CHAPTER 12
Epilogue: Eight Means Whole

Eight years. That's how long it's been since I looked in the mirror and saw death staring back. Eight years since I decided life was still worth fighting for.

I didn't choose the number; God did. I didn't even know back then that eight means new beginnings. All I knew was I was tired—tired of losing, tired of lying, tired of dying with my eyes open.

Now when I write the number 8, it looks like what it is—a loop that never ends. One line flowing into another, no break, no corners. That's how grace feels. Endless.

People always ask, "What keeps you going?" I tell them, "Memory and mercy."

Memory reminds me where I came from. Mercy reminds me why I can't go back.

Every scar I carry, every story I tell, every woman who whispers thank you after hearing me speak—that's fuel. That's purpose.

I'm not chasing fame; I'm chasing impact. I want somebody reading this right now to close this book and whisper, If she can do it, I can too.

Eight years ago, my prayers were just a few words: Help me, God. Now they're full conversations. We talk like family. Sometimes I don't even say "Amen." We just keep the line open all day.

I thank Him while I'm cooking, while I'm driving, while I'm packing orders. Because every simple task used to feel impossible when my mind was chained. Now it's worship.

I've learned that wholeness doesn't mean perfect. It means present.

It means waking up in your right mind and saying, "Today, I'll live like I'm already forgiven."

It means laughing again without checking who's watching. It means crying without shame. It means being gentle with yourself on the days healing feels slow.

Wholeness is balance—strong enough to stand, soft enough to kneel.

The number eight also looks like infinity, and that's what freedom feels like: endless room to breathe. Some days I still hear echoes of the past, but they don't own the microphone anymore. They're background noise to a brand-new melody—faith humming through every corner of my life.

I keep one photo on my dresser: me and my twins at the park, both of them laughing so hard their cheeks looked like sunshine.

When mornings get heavy, I touch that picture and whisper, "We made it, babies."

Because we did. They live through every woman I reach, every child I help, every life I touch. Love didn't die; it just changed form.

If I could talk to the younger me—the scared foster girl, the hurting mother, the woman trying to fill the hole in her heart—I'd tell her this:

You're going to make it. You won't believe it while it's happening, but one day you'll thank God for not answering the prayers that would've ruined you. Keep breathing. Keep fighting. Keep talking to Him even when you think He's quiet. You are not forgotten. You are becoming.

When I travel to speak, I carry a little notebook. On the first page it says: "Eight means whole." On the last page it says: "Keep going."

That's my entire theology in two sentences.

Because life after deliverance is still life—bills, heartbreak, deadlines, delays—but now it comes with direction. I don't wander; I walk.

I used to think survival was the goal. Now I know joy is. Survival keeps you breathing. Joy reminds you why.

So I choose joy—on purpose, every single day. It's my rebellion against everything that tried to silence me.

I don't know what chapter you're in right now, whoever's holding this book. Maybe you're still in the storm. Maybe you're in the slow climb out. Maybe you're finally seeing sunlight but don't trust it yet.

Wherever you are, remember this: God doesn't write tragedies without sequels. f you're reading this, your story's still being written.

Turn the page.

Eight years ago, I whispered, Help me. Today, I shout, Use me. And He does. Every day. In ways I never imagined.

So here's to new beginnings that never end. To every woman finding her voice. To every man fighting his demons in silence. To every mother who thought she'd never smile again. To every child still waiting on rescue— hold on. Love is coming.

I'm whole. Not spotless, not finished, but whole. And that's enough.

Thank You, God, for finding me before I even knew I was lost. Thank You for turning crack smoke into clarity, pain into purpose, shame into strength, and silence into song. Thank You for eight years—and forever more.

Because now I know: Eight means whole.

ACKNOWLEDGMENTS

First and always, I thank God.

If you've read my story, you already know why.
He found me when I wasn't even looking for Him.
He carried me when I couldn't stand, loved me when I
couldn't love myself, and turned every piece of my pain
into proof that His mercy never misses.

To my son, thank you for standing beside me,
working with me, and believing in the business we built
together when it was just an idea and a prayer.
To my two beautiful twin boys in Heaven, thank you for
being my angels and my motivation. You keep me
grounded, guided, and going.

To Mylia Jaza—thank you for helping me see
myself as more, for pushing me to start my business with
my son, and for making sure I got this book out this year.
You reminded me that my story had power even when I
was too tired to believe it.

To my friends, foes, and family members, thank
you for every word, every doubt, every silence, and every

lesson. You can already tell from my story what I want to thank each of you for. Every experience—good, bad, and in-between—became a stepping stone toward the woman I am today.

To my readers, thank you for opening this book and giving me your time, your mind, and your heart. You didn't just read my truth—you carried it. I pray that something in these pages reminds you that God can use anybody.

And finally, to my aunt—thank you for hurting me more than I could have ever imagined the night you were supposed to just babysit. That pain became power. That wound became wisdom. You gave me life experiences that have now inspired two books, and the tell-all is next—for you to finally get that shine you've always wanted. You might not want it by the time I'm finished, but you'll finally have it.

To everyone in my family who turned their backs on me and talked bad about me, to the friends and colleagues who counted me out—thank you. All of you helped push me so low that I couldn't help but rise.

And rise I did.

THE ART & ARTIST

Yogyrl Diamond has heard it all — "crackhead," "junkie," "unfit mother." But after surviving everything from childhood separation and abuse to the murder of her twins, she's done apologizing.

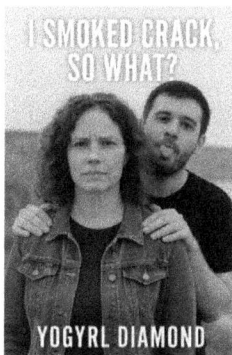

In I Smoked Crack, So What?, Yogyrl speaks for every woman who's been pushed to the edge, called out of her name, and forced to fight for her dignity. This isn't another pity-party recovery story. It's the unapologetic truth of a woman who found God outside the walls of AA and NA, on her own knees, with her own tears — and who decided to live free, clean, and fearless.

From foster homes to street corners, from heartbreak to healing, Yogyrl's voice is raw, unfiltered, and full of faith. She's not asking for forgiveness or approval. She's demanding respect.

This is not a story about addiction.
It's a story about resurrection.

💬 Excerpt / Opening Monologue

They still whisper when I walk in a room.

"Ain't that the one who used to smoke crack?"

Yeah, that was me — used to.

I smoked crack, so what? I don't anymore. And if that's all you can say about me after everything God's brought me through, then that says more about you than it ever will about me.

I'm not a victim. Not anymore. I don't go to meetings to remind myself of who I was. I stay in prayer to thank God for who I am now.

We got abused. We got scarred. We grew up broken. But somehow, we all found each other again as grown folks — eight kids who made it out of different hells with different scars.

Published with assistance from BePublished.org, I SMOKED CRACK, SO WHAT? by Yogyrl Diamond is available as an eBook and softcover from online and bricks-and-mortar book retailers including your favorite bookstore.

THE AUTHOR

Yogyrl Diamond is a California native now living in Ohio. A bold survivor and first-time author, she writes with the same raw honesty that carried her through life's hardest lessons.

Once caught in the cycle of addiction, loss, and judgment, Yogyrl found her freedom in faith — not through meetings or mantras, but through a real relationship with God. Her debut book, I Smoked Crack, So What?, is her unfiltered testimony and her declaration of victory over shame.

Today, she uses her voice to empower others to face their truth, reclaim their power, and walk proudly in who they've become.

Yogyrl Diamond is a California native now living in Ohio. A proud mother, businesswoman, and first-time author, she writes with the same honesty that helped her break every chain meant to hold her down.

"I'm not who I was," she proudly admits. "And, that's exactly why I'm speaking."

Yogyrl lost everything but her faith — and that was enough to rebuild her whole life. No pity. No excuses. Just truth.

"You can't shame a woman who's already faced her demons and lived," she warns her tormentors.

"That's why I'm so proud of her, and we've been able to support each other and achieve things that will make sure we will always be okay no matter what," her son, Roddy Danger, confesses.

Although they didn't go into details, the mother and son team did say they do the work others won't do. It is because of finding this niche in the market that their lives changed virtually after one week.

"Because their ego is too large to handle the shit we do," Yogyrl said.

She added that everyone they'd told the business plan to didn't believe it would work. Once the business got up and going, when people found out what they do, they look down on them despite the high income their businesses nets.

But, Yogyrl and her son don't let the insults get to them. They just keep achieving personal and professional goals, including making sure Yogyrl releases her debut literary work, I SMOKE CRACK SO WHAT?

Her debut memoir is her unapologetic testimony of faith, redemption, and self-respect. It tells the story of a woman who refused to be defined by addiction, pain, or judgment—and instead found peace, purpose, and power in God.

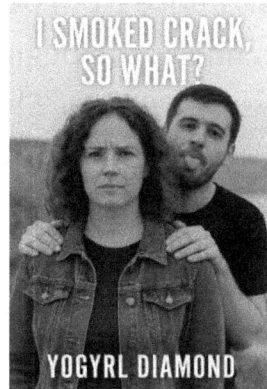

When she's not writing or running her growing business with her son, Yogyrl inspires others through public speaking, mentorship, and daily acts of grace. Her life's mission is to help others rise from ro ck bottom to real freedom, proving that no past is too dark for God to light.

I Smoked Crack, So What? was published with assistance from BePublished.org in November 2025 and stands as the beginning of Yogyrl's literary journey. She's already preparing her next release—the highly anticipated tell-all follow-up that continues her fearless storytelling and truth-telling legacy.

Yogyrl Diamond lives by this truth: "You can't shame a woman who's already faced her demons and lived."She is also working on helping her son record and release his music, and publish his book that's a companion work to his EP project. This work will be released in 2026 if it is not released before 2025 ends.

www.ingramcontent.com/pod-product-compliance
Lightning Source LLC
Chambersburg PA
CBHW060542100426

42742CB00013B/2418